Bulldozers

by Peter Brady

Bridgestone Books
an Imprint of Capstone Press

Bridgestone Books are published by Capstone Press
818 North Willow Street, Mankato, Minnesota 56001

Library of Congress Cataloging-in-Publication Data
Brady, Peter.
Bulldozers/Peter Brady
    p. cm.
Includes bibliographical references and index.
Summary: Introduces bulldozers by describing their parts, the function of each part, the
work bulldozers do, and how they work with other machines.
ISBN 1-56065-351-5
1. Bulldozers--Juvenile literature. [1. Bulldozers.] I. Title.
TA725.B68 1996
629.225--dc20
                                    95-47781
                                       CIP
                                       AC

Photo credits

Unicorn/Eric R. Berndt: cover, 12
Unicorn/David P. Dill: 4, 16
Unicorn/John L. Ebeling: 18
Unicorn/Jean Higgins: 10
Unicorn/Martha McBride: 8
Joe Staudenbaur: 6, 14, 20

Table of Contents

Words in **boldface** type in the text are defined in the Words to Know section in the back of this book.

Bulldozers

Bulldozers are earthmovers. They push, rip, and scrape the ground. They are often the first machines used to build a road or a building.

Bulldozer Parts

Some bulldozers are big and some are small. The two main parts of a bulldozer are the tracks and the blade. Some bulldozers have rippers, too.

Tracks

Bulldozers move on wide steel tracks. The tracks work like **snowshoes**. They let the bulldozer work in wet and muddy areas where wheels would sink.

Spurs

Some tracks are covered with raised steel pieces. These pieces are called spurs. The tracks and spurs break up earth and rock.

Controlling the Tracks

A bulldozer's tracks are controlled by hand levers or foot pedals. The right and left tracks are controlled, separately. One track can move forward while the other track moves backward. That way, the bulldozer can make sharp turns.

The Blade

The blade is a big piece of steel on the front of the bulldozer. The blade is curved. It scoops the earth and pushes it away.

The Ripper

Some bulldozers have a ripper. It is a big metal spike on the back of the bulldozer. It breaks up the earth so the blade can move it.

Reshaping the Earth

People want to change the shape of the earth when they make new roads, buildings, and golf courses. They draw plans showing the changes. The bulldozer moves the earth until it looks like the plans.

Working with Other Machines

Earthmoving is the bulldozer's special job. It works with other machines that have their own special jobs. Some of the machines it works with are **backhoes, front-end loaders, graders,** and dump trucks.

Hands On: Dirt You Can Eat

You will need:
    4 tablespoons (60 milliliters) butter
    8 ounces (224 grams) cream cheese
    8 ounces (224 grams) whipped topping
    1/2 cup (.12 liters) powdered sugar
    1-1/2 small boxes instant vanilla pudding
    2 cups (.48 liter) milk
    1-1/2 pounds (.68 kilogram) chocolate sandwich
    cookies.

1. In a large bowl, mix all ingredients except cookies.
2. Crush the cookies to look like dirt.
3. Put 3/4 of the cookie crumbs in a 9x13-inch pan.
4. Spread the cream mixture on top.
5. Cover with the rest of the crumbs.
6. Put in the refrigerator until cold.
7. Add gummy worms to the dirt and eat.

Words to Know

backhoe—a digging machine with a bucket at the end of a long arm

front-end loader—a machine with a big bucket that picks up piles of material

grader—a machine with a huge blade that smooths out the earth

snowshoes—wood frames strung with strips of leather. Snowshoes are worn under the shoes to keep the feet from sinking in deep snow.

Read More

Hennessy, B.G. *Road Builders.* New York: Viking, 1994.

Kalman, Bobbie and Petrina Gentile. *Dirt Movers.* New York: Crabtree, 1994.

Llewellyn, Claire. *Truck.* New York: Dorling Kindersley, 1995.

Royston, Angela. *Big Machines.* New York: Little, Brown, 1994.

Index